MY NAME WILL GROW WIDE LIKE A TREE

MY
NAME
WILL
GROW
WIDE
LIKE
A TREE

Selected Poems

Yi Lei

Translated from the Chinese by
Tracy K. Smith and Changtai Bi

Graywolf Press

Grateful acknowledgment is made to the editors of the following journals,
who first published versions of these translations: *The Bennington Review*:
Love's Dance 4, 6, 7 & 10; *Circumference*: A Single Woman's Bedroom,
Picnic; *Harper's Magazine*: Red Wall; *Harvard Review*: Love's Dance 1, 3
& 9; *New Poetry from China 1917–2017*: Flesh; *The New Yorker*: Flame in the
Cloud at Midnight; *Poetry East West*: Flesh; *The Slowdown*: Flesh.

This publication is made possible, in part, by the voters of Minnesota
through a Minnesota State Arts Board Operating Support grant, thanks to
a legislative appropriation from the arts and cultural heritage fund. Signifi-
cant support has also been provided by Target Foundation, the McKnight
Foundation, the Lannan Foundation, the Amazon Literary Partnership, and
other generous contributions from foundations, corporations, and individu-
als. To these organizations and individuals we offer our heartfelt thanks.

MINNESOTA
STATE ARTS BOARD

CLEAN
WATER
LAND &
LEGACY
AMENDMENT

Special funding for this book was provided by Edwin C. Cohen.

Published by Graywolf Press
250 Third Avenue North, Suite 600
Minneapolis, Minnesota 55401

www.graywolfpress.org

Published in the United States of America
Printed in Canada

ISBN 978-1-64445-040-6

2 4 6 8 9 7 5 3 1
First Graywolf Printing, 2020

Library of Congress Control Number: 2019956913

Cover design: Kyle G. Hunter

Cover art: George Peters / Digital Vision Vectors / Getty Images

CONTENTS

目次

INTRODUCTION

Yi Lei (伊蕾) astounded readers in China when, in 1987, she published a long poem entitled "A Single Woman's Bedroom." In it, a female speaker expresses her passion and sexual desire. Again and again, she returns to the refrain "You didn't come to live with me" as she laments her lover's failure to make good on his promise—this at a time when cohabitation before marriage was still illegal in China. The poem goes further still, laying claim to a freedom of the mind and spirit, and openly criticizing the rigidity of law:

> I imagine a life in which I possess
> All that I lack. I fix what has failed.
> What never was, I build and seize.
> It's impossible to think of everything,
> Yet more and more I do. Thinking
> What I am afraid to say keeps fear
> And fear's twin, rage, at bay. Law
> Squints out from its burrow, jams
> Its quiver with arrows. It shoots
> Like it thinks: never straight. My thoughts
> Escape.

In other poems, Yi Lei writes as movingly of grief as of love, of joy as of deep unrest. She celebrates and aligns herself with nature—as in this line from "Green Trees Greet the Rainstorm": "I belong to the nation of wild arms flailing in the wind." In "Besieged" her vision moves nimbly from the earthbound and everyday to the cosmic, the enduring:

> What binds the boundless?
> Our tiny minds will come to grief
> Trying to imagine what lies past it.
> Unfathomable. To ponder it
> Will cost me no small wedge of eternity,
> But for that time I'll be boundless.

Still not yet widely translated into English, Yi Lei's work came to me almost by happenstance. In December 2013, I received word from Yuanyang Wang, a Chinese poet and translator, that a poet friend of his would be visiting New York City and would like to meet. A month later, I had lunch in Chinatown with Yi Lei and her friend Nancy Bumin, who, being the only one of us conversant in both Mandarin and English, served as our liaison. It was a cold January afternoon, coincidentally the first day of the Chinese New Year.

I'd been given a rough translation of "A Single Woman's Bedroom," and I'd been drawn into the expansive sweep of it. The poem is made up of fourteen related sections that follow almost improvisationally from one another, each driven by a sharp emotional insistence. I felt admiration for this poet's passion, her sense of play, the ways each new gesture brought in a new gust of energy and indelible imagery. Her poem's relentless availability to love, even in the wake of betrayal or devastation, spoke to feelings of desire, resistance, and loss that live in and have instigated a number of my own poems.

"Would it be okay," I'd asked Nancy to ask Yi Lei, "if in certain of my translations, instead of being faithful to the literal features of the poem, I sought to build a similar spirit or feeling for readers of American English?"

There was some back and forth in Mandarin. "Yes," was the eventual answer.

"I want to make the reader feel at home in these poems. Would it be okay if certain details were to shift or be replaced with others rooted in this culture?"

Again, there was more back and forth across the table. And then Nancy told me that Yi Lei was comfortable with my making these kinds of nuanced choices.

We weren't even midway through our long New Year's lunch, yet I was brimming with joy at the prospect of living awhile in the vision and vocabulary of these poems and this imagination. Yi Lei trusted me to live with and respond to her poems, and to offer them to readers in the way that I heard and felt them. It was a remarkable freedom and a daunting responsibility. And, yes, I was already committed to the task of shepherding this indispensable voice into a living contemporary English.

Four years later, I took my first trip to visit Yi Lei in China. My flight landed in Beijing hours late, and I moved slowly, with a battery of tired travelers, through customs and immigration. It was nearly two o'clock in the morning, but Yi Lei and my cotranslator, Changtai Bi (who goes by the name David), were waiting to welcome me. Of Yi Lei's hospitality during that visit, all I can say is that I thought my heart would burst from gratitude at the beautiful entrée into her world that she'd provided, for it was with a quiet exuberance that she afforded me a glimpse into China's complex past and its many-layered present. Most emphatically, spending a week in Beijing allowed me to get to know Yi Lei in her own element, with her peers and protégés, friends and family; to see her negotiating her city and decoding her own history for an eager guest. I recognized in her person the largeness of spirit, the agelessness, the fearless availability to experience, and the inner nobility that animate her poems.

Happiest are the brief flashes of memory: holding her hand as we hurried along a bustling block; her pointing my attention to people, foods, and architecture signaling a way of life now all but gone. We spent my last afternoon in Beijing with her niece, Yisha, pulling canvases down from the many racks of the studio where Yi Lei lived and, in recent years, made paintings. In the last three decades of her life, Yi Lei painted hundreds of beautiful and arresting figurative canvases: probing self-portraits; series upon series of roses, peonies, and lilies which speak to states of joy, loss, and transcendence. I came away with yet another understanding of the vast self to which she gave voice in her poems.

Once, over dinner and with David translating, Yi Lei told me the story of the great love that inspired "A Single Woman's Bedroom." In our twenty-first-century shorthand, I will say, simply: *it was complicated*. I envied Yi Lei's ability to claim the fact of that love, and to embrace the joy and upheaval it led to without apologizing for it or turning against it as is sometimes the case when one looks back at the many detours of one's own youth. "Love is innocent," she said. And with that simple phrase, I believe she explained parts of myself to me, which is, of course, what great poets do.

The last time we met, six months later, Yi Lei offered me feedback on my translation of "A Single Woman's Bedroom." In particular, she wanted me to attend better to the poem's later sections, which I had initially translated with too much emphasis upon romantic love. She wanted me to see that her poem turns from a fixation upon the liberation of sensual love to an urgent insistence upon the individual's freedom from unjust institutions. The pined-for beloved, as the poem progresses, is no longer a man, but an essential concept. And the disappointment driving the poem is leveraged finally, and importantly, against the self. "A Single Woman's Bedroom" concludes with these lines:

14. *Hope Beyond Hope*

This city of riches has fallen empty.
Small rooms like mine are easy to breach.
Watchmen pace, peer in, gazes hungry.
I come and go, always alone, heavy with worry.
My flesh forsakes itself. Strangers' eyes
Drill into me till I bleed. I beg God:
Make me a ghost.
            Fellow citizens:
Something invisible blocks every road.
I wait night after night with a hope beyond hope.
If you come, will nation rise against nation?
If you come, will the Yellow River drown its banks?
If you come, will the sky blacken and rage?
Will your coming decimate the harvest?
There is nothing I can do in the face of all I hate.
What I hate most is the person I've become.
            You didn't come to live with me.

Yi Lei died suddenly in the summer of 2018 while traveling in Europe. She was and remains a revolutionary voice in Chinese poetry. I feel immensely fortunate to be able to say, from firsthand knowledge, that she was huge-hearted and philosophical, on intimate terms with the world in the way of Walt Whitman, one of her literary heroes.

This volume was nearing completion when David startled me with the terrible news of Yi Lei's death. We had spent part of the previous autumn in Beijing discussing the progress I'd made with her poems. Our manner of collaborating was this: working from David's literal translation of a manuscript of Yi Lei's poems, I would listen to the poem's statements and the images—essentially trying to visualize the poem's realm, and to align myself with the feeling and logic of the work. Then, I'd attempt to re-envision and re-situate these things in English. Occasionally, this was a matter of shifting toward smoother, more active, evocative language. Often, it entailed locating a relationship between verbs and nouns and aligning those features within a new metaphor or image system, as occurred in this passage from David's literal translation of "Love's Dance":

> When you quietly evaded
> It seemed that land sank in front of the chest
> My shout was blocked by echoes
> It was invisible hands that forged my mistake
> To avoid a pitiful tragedy
> I strangled the freedom of souls
>> To let my reason be pitch-black from then
>> I am willing to be dominated by you

I allowed *land sank, blocked, echoes, forged, tragedy,* and *pitch-black* to guide me toward the metaphor of mining, which resulted in this passage from my version of the poem:

> What happened deep in the mountain of me.
> And then the mine in collapse. The shaft

Choked with smoke. Voice burying voice.
An absence of air, preponderance of pitch.
I don't want to know, or understand, or be restored
To reason. In the wake of certain treasons, I am
    Still domitable, a claim in wait. I am
    Possessed of my depths. I am willing still.

My strategy, whenever I reached a point of hesitation, was to ask the surrounding features of the poem to suggest a continuity that might guide me forward. Sometimes, I'd make a leap of faith, trusting to the larger energetic pull of the poem to keep me from losing the trail. Then I'd send my work to David, who would translate it back into Chinese for Yi Lei. Yi Lei read my version for feeling, image, and intention. If she recognized in my poem something essential from her original, we let things stand. Our conversation took place back and forth in this triangulated fashion.

I have sought, in my translations of Yi Lei's poems, to cleave to the original spirit, tone, and impetus. But it is important to recognize that often they do so by veering away from the vocabulary, or occasionally the form, of the original. In addition to the literal deviations described above, I also accepted the fact that the music of the original—which I wasn't capable of recognizing in the Chinese, or gleaning from David's intermediary translation—could not be a component of my concerns as a translator. What I hope emerges clearly for readers in English is some of the rhythmic and emotional insistence of Yi Lei's use of statement, repetition, and refrain.

I trust that this bilingual selection of Yi Lei's poems will allow readers of both languages to grasp and assess the choices I've made in the translations, while also presenting the original work in its own terms. Across the English and the Chinese, readers will hear, perhaps more than anything, the conversation that took shape between Yi Lei's poetics and my own. Perhaps that conversation will, in turn, embolden someone to translate these poems based on other principles, giving them new forms of existence and further enlivening the conversation about the work of this brilliant and essential poet.

I offer tremendous and ongoing thanks to my cotranslator David—Changtai Bi—for his good humor, generosity, and tireless work in ferrying versions of these poems back and forth across languages. David's long friendship with Yi Lei has been a source of insight and consolation indispensable to the completion of this volume.

Tracy K. Smith
Princeton, New Jersey

MY NAME WILL GROW WIDE LIKE A TREE

GREEN TREES GREET THE RAINSTORM

I belong to the nation of wild arms flailing in wind.
And I know you are bound to unravel me, but how can I not
Lift my head and look you in the eye? How can I fail to greet you,
    Though my living gown will soon be battered to threads?
    Better this lashing—flesh burst open, ransacked by air—
    Than to live ambushed by loneliness.

I belong to the nation of startled cries, voices flailing in wind.
And I know you are bound to unravel me, but how can I not
Lift my head and look you in the eye? How can I fail to greet you,
    Though my living gown will soon be shredded, shed?
    Better to be ravaged straightaway in youth
    Than to live out another year's quiet undoing.

                                    July 30, 1982

HUANGGUOSHU WATERFALL

Great stones of whitewater
                            hammer down
Onto our unhurried walk in the monument's shade,
And our cramped bed at the "Vienna Villa"
And the gloomy rooms where no one spoke.
Great stones of whitewater hammer
Onto the statue of a woman made of moon-white wax
And the thatchy backwater island with its haunted stretch
Of hotel corridor. Great stones of whitewater
Smashing what I didn't ask on the lip of the ancient tomb.
Smashing what you nevertheless couldn't give.
Smashing the little apple tree growing happily in sand
Like a souvenir painting. Those red drapes, that weepy guitar.
Smashing your hesitation on the shore.
Great stones of whitewater hammering, hammering down—
Eviscerate me.
My soul won't plant itself in this deep black soil,
Recoils from eternity, like a thief. No,
My soul hangs with all that water, thousands of years' worth
Roiling away
                Up on the edge of that cliff.

                                        September 20, 1985

4

BETWEEN STRANGERS

Stranger, who can measure the distance between us?
Distance is the rumor of a never-before-seen sea.
Distance the width of a layer of dust.
Maybe we need only strike a match
for my world to flicker in your sky,
Visible finally, and eye-to-eye.
Breachable, finally, the border between us.
What if we touched? What then?
Would something in us hum an old familiar song?
Maybe then our feet would wear a path back and forth
between our lives, like houses in neighboring lots.
Would you give me what I lack? Your winter coat,
Your favorite battered pot? Logic warns: unlikely.
History tells me to guard my distance
When I pass you on the street, and I obey.
But—to stumble into you, or you into me—
Wouldn't it be sweet? In reality,

I keep to myself. You keep to you. We have nothing
To rue. So why does remorse rise almost to my brim,
And also in you?

1985

PICNIC

Daylight tumbles down the grassy hill
Where we feast on spiced fish,
And the whiskers speckling your chin.

    Why not let your beard go long, shambolic
    Like a sage or savage?
    Just once, I'd like to be savage . . .

Oh, let's eat, let's eat!
Let's guzzle down expensive wine
And buttered black bread.

Let's eat your hands, lifting off like astonished birds
And your hair, dark as an owl's shadow.
Let's eat your teeth, teeming with laughter.
Let's eat until even the sun is eaten, and all that are left

Are those clouds circling on wide white wings
Which we wouldn't dream of eating.

                  March 5, 1986

FURTIVE

A black squall blankets the earth.
The stubborn are drenched, worn down.
Even dreams are slick and choked with moss.

Is meeting out of habit any worse
Than coming clean? I can't let go
Of this clipping lifted from your wife's garden.

Time and again, my voice storms up in a rage,
Weeps back down in tatters.
Such secrecy unravels me. Still,
My heart harbors a furtive joy.
(Why must I whisper?)

I've been careless with your letters, which lie scattered,
Lost. My name for you creeps off
Like a plant that has overgrown its pot.

June 15, 1986

LOVE'S DANCE

1. *It was a bewitching*

It was a bewitching, your open hand
Motionless, mute, but resolute,
Commanding. Of course I followed, past
Lights first dim, then sordid—bright
As a marquee of the underworld.
Your animal heat, heart in full gallop.
I gripped you with my heels, fingers
Knotted into your hair. I saw my blue coat
Transformed into a dune-colored cape.
Day and night. That urge and charge. Then
I got down and accepted the bit.
I, for whom solitude was as vast as the prairie!
      Loving you shed light on the catastrophes of history.
      Still, certain questions continue to saddle me.

2. *Tango*

Tango—fervent, feverish—
Rises and swells. The dancers'
Fanfarrón saws at me, splitting
My left leg from my right,
Lopping my lifetime
like a halved melon.
Footsteps echo,
Divided. And voices.
All I've done, thought,
The song sung softly
In my heart. Cut. Stop.
Contrapasso. The dance
Scissors you, too. It aches,
This fate, this wish

To hook and glide.
You are a unity,
I am a unity, but once
We were an aboriginal *we*,
Hacked in two by a tactless deity.
> Our wish since forever: to be
> Re-fused, unsevered.

3. *I don't want to be restored to reason*

Music falls measure by measure
To the floor, but desire is a striptease
Performed in reverse. The heart's ore
Buried miles deep, and for what?
I shrink even from myself. I wish
To get out from under the sky,
Which handles me with an infuriating
Familiarity. But that day—your hand—
What happened deep in the mountain of me.
And then the mine in collapse. The shaft
Choked with smoke. Voice burying voice.
An absence of air, preponderance of pitch.
I don't want to know, or understand, or be restored
To reason. In the wake of certain treasons, I am
> Still domitable, a claim in wait. I am
> Possessed of my depths. I am willing still.

4. *What is death that anyone should fear it?*

When the crowd scatters
Like leaves in wind, I stay.
The sun is that red, that
Solicitous. And then there's you
Casting shadows so portentous
My soul wants to cower,

Scamper, scuttle. I'm befuddled.
You are distinct. I am distinct.
But if I can't reach your arm,
The plane of your cheek—or if
You can't lean in to inspect
The tender vessel of my eye—
I can't help it; I want to cry.
Passion rolls in, blinding
As fog, and just as cold. There are
High cliffs in the distance, chalk white,
Beyond which roils an icy, jagged sea.
What is death that anyone should
Fear it? When you're near, you
Open your mouth and a fence
Plants itself in rock. The sirens—
Voices so pure they could save me
From the anguish of the real—
        Are silenced by the pleasure
        Of our talk.

5. *Naked, alive*

Like search lights, our lines of sight collide
Naked, alive, refusing to hide.
All struggle is futile. Left or right?
How would I leave this labyrinth of rubble?
And whom do I tax with my burden of being lost?
Ahead is the black swirl of what I'll never see,
Which also follows me.
Music, though, is an infinity, even
If any instant it will end. And there's your gaze,
Dragging the plane, scurrying me into whichever pit.
        Let me die quickly and gripped by the opposite of regret.

6. *I'm liquid*

Capri.
Liquid rhythm shimmers
In afternoon light. I am
This island's daughter,
A rock in water.
At dusk,
I spread myself
Across the distances
Crying into wet air. Pain
Wakes and dances for you.
Pain peels back my clothes,
Bares my skin made taut
By the idea of your hands.
Wolf. Wild dog. When you
Flash the fresh blade
Of your smile, or
When you sink into me
Like a hook, I think
  The greatest of joys
  Must be reserved
  For the weak.

7. *Such a word as* friend

I haven't yet memorized your steps,
Though my hair lurches to learn,
Leaps up like a shameless dancer.
If there is such a word as *friend*,
Whose mouth does it fit in? The world's
Mouth curls up in fear when it sees
Where we're leading it, shuts its eyes.
I think of you, friend, and go blurry.
Would you be able to tell me

Whether there is just the one moon caught
In the net of sky, or if that's another—there—
Skimming the water like an impostor?
And how can I not swim through your veins,
A fish in your river? Maybe *friend*
Is contested territory. Not like *lover*,
Which once was but now is over.
Friend remains a mystery, like everything
That once stirred me. I would rather
You were someone else entirely. Not you,
Nor the recollection of you. The moon
Smirks at its twin, noncommittal. Oh,
And the dance I said my hair was doing?
I think now it must just have been
   Lost in reflection.

8. *Centripetal. Central.*

Radius. Radius.
We are the cross-
Bar of a living star
Whose every facet
Burns. A glory.
Spin and whorl.
Hurl and turn.
Centripetal. Central.
Centered over the eye
Of the center, that teeming,
Living core. I have no idea
What we've got
In our orbit, what may
Crush us like rubbish.
It snowed here once
In the mountains in June.
The white flakes rushed us

With the frenzy of new love.
But that was a lifetime ago.
June has sweltered ever since.

9. *I fight with myself*

I am on my way, on my way to you,
Striding the earth, it seems, the tundra
Between us, though I am nearing you now,
Nearing the tropics of your chest, that island
Around which the water rolls and swells.
Time gapes wide like a cavern.
I fight with myself, am yanked back.
You villain touch! what are you doing?
I was so angry once, a bay of hostility.
What if I stop now and let myself be
Lapped against like a barrier of rocks? Not
The sharp-edged gnarled ones that wink
Out beyond the borders of safety, but
          The gentle ones that sleep here
          Chastely in a little heap.

10. *I love disco*

If you are prowling the tall grass
Where I graze, I want you
To crouch down low and let your tail
Twitch for a moment in hope.

Let me feel the wind in my fur,
Gnats tickling my ears.
How I love to see the earth
Curving away in all directions,

To plant my hooves, nose
The leaves, certain as civilization
That I will last! Inching closer:
The threat of your heat, your shadow

Grows to blot me out like ink.
Once in a dream I let a man
Stencil my face with purple clematis
And Japanese painted fern. I woke

And froze, afraid to look. Then I gladdened,
Recalling the beast of you that might,
       Any moment, thunder up from behind
       With a hunger drawn from deep in the earth.

11. *Let's wander*

The soundtrack tonight's
So somber. Come on,
Let's wander. We'll
Lose ourselves
In every direction. Trees,
Shade, wind in the valley.
Or street corners,
Anonymous alleys.
Let's wander
Then lie down together.
Come flood, come mob,
Come resurrection fire.
Come on, let's wander
Farther, wider.
The days are long,
And what pushes back
Is strong and never tires.

Wandering (Sunday)
Wandering (Monday)
Wandering (Tuesday)
Wandering (Wednesday)
Wandering (Thursday)
Wandering (Friday)
Wandering (Saturday)

12. *Already gone*

Weary, wary, watching you
Watch me. Your gale-force gaze
Wants to topple me. I give.
This dance of lunge and tug,
Touch and—*oh!* My dress:
A snake in coils on the rug.

The sad, old joke of it is this:
I don't yet know what you want,
What I'll be called upon to grieve,
But I know this bliss
Will leave. Why? And when?
      I can almost see past the blaze
      Of what dawns to the charred
      Husk of it already gone.

13. *Uncrowned Incorruptible*

God strikes his holy bells—*Ave Maria!*—and
Your hand grabs mine. We, the uncrowned Righteous,
The uncrowned Incorruptible, mute of vows and
Ignorant of commandments. Our practiced restraint
Has earned us what? How many Sundays lived

In vain? There are laws and there is Law. There is love
And there is Love; Need and a nagging small want.
I would be happy to forsake everything they told me
To desire: glory, rejoicing, even death. To be left
With only a limitless holy blank. And you?

Do you remember our Old Testament phase,
Quaking at the fate of whole cities abruptly erased?
Now we're onto Jesus—those feet! those wrists!—
Though belief is a country that eludes us.
For ceremony, we light a mosquito coil,

Turn down the bed, whisper about small things
Like mornings on the beach, swimming farther
And farther into cold rhythmic waves, almost
Eager for the greedy underside of day.
God is ravenous unending fright.

> Blessed Virgin, safe on the shore, or high up
> On the cliff overlooking every sea: forget me.

14. *Until my breast blared with industry*

I had been dreaming
Of dancing—just us two,

Here, where threat
Is the very weather

And tragedy
A soaring currency.

You lifted your arms,
Locked them around me

Until my breast blared
With industry.

Sky, solid ground,
Firmaments so far off

Yet so real. I want to feel
Civilization flourish and fall.

And I want to live to tell.

·Let bodies go to Heaven!
Let souls go to Hell!

15. *A swan cries out in the dusk*

Dim light dances
On the bare wall
Like music
At a wedding. Candle-

Light on the wall
Says *They Do, They Will,
They May*, tells law
And oath to go away.

Tomorrow is a shy bride.
Today passes dutifully by.
Before I am too old,
I should like to have a picnic

Alone on the young grass
Alongside the river.
And then—
And then?

Our frail light dims.
A presence we can't see
Skims past, watching.
We fail to kiss.

A swan cries out
In the dusk. It is tempting
To believe something
Significant is ending.

    It is.

16. *Destination gave chase*

A bewitching, yes.
I surrendered my bearings,
Was flagrant in my forgetting.

Wherever I ought to have been
Going was mere distraction,
A nagging confusion. I was

Circling around something, yes.
Day, night, unfazed by danger.
I suppose I was heading

Somewhere. But where?
Destination gave chase and,
Merciless, fled. You

Were lost with me, circling
Back and around,
Gaining, ceding ground,

On and on in such a manner.
On and on, getting nowhere
Despite exhaustion, knowing better.

My body, now, is like a paper sack
That has been crumpled
And smoothed flat, creased

Every which way and packed
With sorrow. Why? Why
Has my life gone on so long?

I am ready to set down all of it—
      Today, tomorrow, yesterday—
      To set it down and walk away.

                    Mid-September 1986

A SINGLE WOMAN'S BEDROOM

1. *Mirror Trick*

Of course you know her.
She is one and many,
A multitude flashing on, then off,
Watching out from the blank
Of her face. She is silent, speaking
With just her mind. She is flesh, a form,
But also flat, a mute screen.
What she offers you, by no means
Should you accept. She belongs to no one,
Sitting like a ghost beyond her own reach.
And yet, she's there—I mean *me*—
Behind glass, as if the world has been cleaved,
Though something whole remains,
Roving, free, a voice with poise and pitch.
She's there—*me*—snug in the glass,
The mirror on the bedside
Doing its one trick
A hundred times a day.
          You didn't come to live with me.

2. *Turkish Bath*

The room is choked with nudes.
Once, a man muscled in by mistake
Crying, "Turkish bath!" He had no idea
My door is always locked in this heat,
No idea that I am the sole guest and client,
The chief consort, that I cast my gaze
Of pity and absolute pride across
The length of my limbs—pristine, lithe—
The bells of my breasts singing,

The high bright note of my ass,
My shoulders a warm chord,
The chorus of muscle that rings
Ecstatic. I am my own model.
I create, am created, my bed
Is heaped with photo albums,
Socks and slips scattered on a table.
A spray of winter jasmine wilts
In its glass vase, dim yellow, like
Despondent gold. Blossoms carpet
The floor, which is a patchwork
Of pillows. Pick a corner, sleep in peace.
        You didn't come to live with me.

3. *The curtain seals in my joy*

The curtain seals out the day.
Better that way to let my mind
See what it sees (every evil under the sun),
Or to kneel before the heart, quiet king,
Feeling brave and consummately free.
Better that way to let all that I want
And all I believe swarm me like bees,
Or ghosts, or a cloud of smoke someone
Blows, beckoning. I come. I cry out
In release. I give birth
To a battery of clever babies—triplets,
Quintuplets, so many all at once.
The curtain seals in my joy.
The curtain holds the razor out of reach,
Puts the pills on a shelf out of sight.
The curtain snuffs shut and I bask in the bounty
Of being alive. The music begins.
Love pools in every corner.
        You didn't come to live with me.

4. Self-Portrait

The camera snaps. Spits me out ugly.
So I set out to paint the self within myself.
It takes twelve tubes, blended to a living tint,
Before I believe me. I name the mixture *Color P*.
The hair—curious, unlikely—is my favorite,
The same fluff of bangs tickling my niece's face.
And my eyebrows are wide as hills. They swallow everything.
They are a feat. They do not impress me as likely to age.
They are brimming with wisdom. Neither slavish nor stern.
Not magnificent, but not the kind made to crumple in shame.
Not prudish. Unwilling to arch and beckon like a whore's.
They skitter away from certainties like *alive* or *dead*.
My self-portrait hangs on the narrow wall,
And I kneel before it every day.
          You didn't come to live with me.

5. Impromptu Party

The table is draped with a festive cloth, and
Light blurs out from a single lamp, making us fuzzy.
A sip of red wine, and I rise to my feet. We are
Dancing, my guests and I, like kids in a ballroom.
We don't smile or even speak.
We've had a lot to drink.
To a single woman, time is like a scrap of meat:
Nothing you can afford to give away. I want
To hold it in my lap, Time, that sneak, that thief already
Scheming to break free. Please—I beg
Upon my beloved stilettos,
I want the world back. I've been alive—could it be?—
Near a century. My face has closed up shop.
My feet are a desolate country.
For a single woman, youth is a feast that lasts

Only until it is gone.
    You didn't come to live with me.

6. *Invitation*

When it arrived, I was interrupted by relief,
Sitting in my rattan chair, feeling the wind ease in
Through the holes in my life.
I only said yes because of his dissertation. Friends,
Nothing more. He talked—about modernism,
Black humor. But always at a remove from reality.
Why didn't he ask me anything?
Tender and petulant, he struck me as cute,
But at heart, only a well-behaved boy.
He offered his arm. Elegant, decent, gallant.
But how can I be a woman
If he is a child? What can come of that union?
Can any of us save ourselves? Save another?
    You didn't come to live with me.

7. *Sunday Alone*

I don't picnic on Sundays.
Parks are a sad song; I steer clear.
But I dug out all my sheet music,
I lolled about in the Turkish bath
Singing from breakfast to dusk.
With my hair, I sang *Do*
And my eyes, *Re*
And my ear sounded *Mi*
And my nose went after *Fa*
My face tilted back and up rose *So*
My mouth breathed *La*
My whole body birthed *Ti*
Like my cousin said, famously—

Music is the soul sighing.
Music pushes back against pain.
Solitude is great (but I don't want
Greatness). My eyes slump
Against the walls. My hair
Hurls itself at the ceiling like a colony
Of bats.

       You didn't come to live with me.

8. *Discourse*

I read materialist philosophy—
Material is peerless.
But I'm creationless.
I don't even procreate.
What use does the world have for me
Here beside my reams of cockeyed drafts
That nick away at the mountain of
Art and philosophy?
Firstly, Existentialism.
Secondly, Dadaism.
Thirdly, Positivism.
Lastly, Surrealism.
Mostly, I think people live
For the sake of living.
Is living a feat?
What will last?
My chief function is obsolescence.
Still, I send out my stubborn breath
In every direction. I am determined
To commit myself to a marriage
Of connivance.

       You didn't come to live with me.

9. *Downpour*

Rain hacks at the earth like an insatiable man.
Disquiet, like passion, subsides instantly.
Six distinct desires mate.
At the moment, I want everything and nothing.
The rainstorm barricaded all the roads. Sandbags.
Isn't there something gladdening about a dead end?
I canceled my plans, my trysts, my escapes.
Stopped the clock that chases me. The clock of the heart, maybe.
It was an ecstasy so profound . . .
      "Ah, linger on, thou art so fair!"
I'd rather admit despair. And die.
      You didn't come to live with me.

10. *Dream of Symbolism*

I occupy the walls that surround me.
When did I become so rectilinear?
I had a rectilinear dream:
The rectilinear sky in Leo:
The head, for a while, shone brightest.
Next the tail. After a while
It became a wild horse
Galloping into the distances of the universe,
Lasso dragging behind, tethered to nothing.
There are no roads in the black night that contains us.
Every step is a step into absence.
I don't remember the last time I saw
A free soul. If she still exists, wild-eyed drifter,
She'll die young.
      You didn't come to live with me.

11. *Birthday Candles*

They are like heaps of stars.
My flat roof is a private galaxy
That stretches on stubbornly forever.
The universe created us by chance,
Our birth, simple happenstance.
Should life be guarded or gambled?
Lodged in a vault or flung to the wind?
God announces: Happy Birthday.
Everyone raises a glass and giggles audibly.
Death gets clearer in the distance. Closer by a year.
Because all are afraid, none is afraid.
A pity how fast youth sputters and burns,
Its flame like the season's last peony.
A bright misery.

  You didn't come to live with me.

12. *Cigarette*

I lift it to my lips, supremely slim,
Igniting my desire to be a woman.
I appreciate the grace of the gesture,
Cosmopolitan, a shorthand for beauty,
The winding haze off the tip like the chaos of sex.
Loneliness can be sweet. I reread the paper.
The ban on smoking underway
Has gotten a bonfire of support. A heated topic,
Though I find it inflammatory. Authority
Flings a struck match in our direction, then
Gasps when we flare into flame. Law:
A contest between lowlifes and sophisticates,
Though only time knows who is who.
Tonight I want to commit a victimless crime.

  You didn't come to live with me.

13. *Thinking*

I spend all my spare time doing it.
I give it a name: walking indoors.
I imagine a life in which I possess
All that I lack. I fix what has failed.
What never was, I build and seize.
It's impossible to think of everything,
Yet more and more I do. Thinking
What I am afraid to say keeps fear
And fear's twin, rage, at bay. Law
Squints out from its burrow, jams
Its quiver with arrows. It shoots
Like it thinks: never straight. My thoughts
Escape. One day, they'll emigrate
To a kingdom far-off and heady.
My visa's in-process, though like anyone,
I worry it's overpopulated already.
       You didn't come to live with me.

14. *Hope Beyond Hope*

This city of riches has fallen empty.
Small rooms like mine are easy to breach.
Watchmen pace, peer in, gazes hungry.
I come and go, always alone, heavy with worry.
My flesh forsakes itself. Strangers' eyes
Drill into me till I bleed. I beg God:
Make me a ghost.
       Fellow citizens:
Something invisible blocks every road.
I wait night after night with a hope beyond hope.
If you come, will nation rise against nation?
If you come, will the Yellow River drown its banks?
If you come, will the sky blacken and rage?

Will your coming decimate the harvest?
There is nothing I can do in the face of all I hate.
What I hate most is the person I've become.
You didn't come to live with me.

Late September 1986

BESIEGED

1. *Subjective*

I'm besieged,
Destined to die grievously.

2. *Nothing anchors me*

I embark on a fugitive journey.
I get off the train, look around.
Nothing anchors me.
The street's not wide, not narrow either
And dull as ditch water.
Its very name advertises a history,
But what of me? Newcomer
From nowhere, why am I here?
Where was I before?
There was a purpose, but
It was nebulous. A kind of death.
Yes, death was the terminus,
But must I let it have me? Must I
Let it have at me gradually?
I wander, aimless. I look up
At the underside of a passing cloud,
So remote in its obedience
To the commanding wind.
Oh, but it is terrible. Unbounded, immense.
I take three breaths then shut my eyes,
Fear my only defense.
Limitless! Limitless! The cosmos
Is immense beyond belief.
What binds the boundless?
Our tiny minds will come to grief
Trying to imagine what lies past it.

Unfathomable. To ponder it
Will cost me no small wedge of eternity,
But for that time I'll be boundless,
And my spirit, accordingly, boundless.
      I'm boundless.

3. *Who am I?*

I click open my compact in sunny grass
And find myself again. Waiting for you to arrive
I strive for universal beauty in bold strokes:
My brows lengthened
My eyes painted wide
My lips red, redder
My lashes stark black.
Who was I born?
Who have I become?
How do shame and glory abide the same face?
For whose benefit, and by what grace, do I obey?
Who am I? And why haven't you come
To see the woman I am,
The one I still seek to become?
Desire is floodwater. I breach
My own highest walls.
      I'm boundless.

4. *I've never quite understood myself*

What color will you paint me?
Yellow? No, absolutely not.
You don't know the tint of my breath,
The shade of my emotions.
My mindset,
My illusions,
My vile predilections—

You've missed them.
You haven't yet seen my colors,
Nor I yours. I'd love to be green,
Like a ghost. Are ghosts green?
Or white, like the angels.
Are angels white? I don't know
What's fearsome, what's
Worthy of worship. I don't
Quite understand myself.
I've never quite understood myself.
      I'm boundless.

5. *The pain of bondage*

The book on my desk is a classic.
Two hours of immersion and
The white page swallows me,
Its prodigious magic stretching
If I rise, shrinking back if I sit.
I move and it follows. No exit.
What an awful trick. To be
Snapped shut, bound,
Pressed in living death. I seek
A window, a door that gives.
I am composing an explosion.
      I'm boundless.

6. *Who is beyond the walls?*

Boxed-in by walls, cut-off
From the sky, bathing inside
What feels like hell, I want
Out suddenly—out!
Who's beyond the walls?
Who's there? Who?

I scramble to rise, don't bother
To rinse or to dry. I can't wait.
I'd rather be caked in mud,
A clay statue lifted from a tomb.
I don't believe in walls. May walls
Cease this very moment to exist.
   I'm boundless.

7. *Dark world*

Your words echo like a chime in this room
With the velvety walls. Your brass tinkling
Besieges me. No road out, no reprieve. I try
To dash through that sound as through a sheet of rain,
But it grows. I take notes, black ink
In a panicked scrawl. Besieged, I sink into
A dark world. I can't lift my feet, I shuffle
Through as though blind. What was it
You explained that we already know? And how
Would you go about proving the reverse?
I wish your voice were made of paper. Thin
Stock. Riddled with a thousand nicks.
   I'm boundless.

8. *Panama blockade*

Sundown, I scour the night market.
It's a language mill, a word factory: Prince
Pants, Toshiba shoes, trendy kicks. I flip
When Panama Pants grip my backside like love,
A siege I bend to gladly, each step a surrender.
Look at me walk, look how they claim me,
Make me already a little more—whose?

Where is Panama? Does it exist? Why must it
Dress us, mess with us, rounding us up for some
Spurious mission? Can I renounce Panama's borders?
Can I cross them? When I'm ready, can I stride away?
      I'm boundless.

9. *Pyramid*

Already the window harbors moonlight
By the time I make it home. My family
Waits like a portrait of a family,
Three sides in deferential seating,
A golden triangle, a pyramid:
Immense, ancient, laden with secrets,
With the ageless silence of its form.

Who is safe? Who must sacrifice? How
Long will the years enslave us?
My limbs are already stiff, my blood
Has chilled. Fame was heavy,
A burden I chose to abandon. Better
Merely to breathe, merely to breathe.
      I'm boundless.

10. *Of consequence uncertain*

I spill secrets in public,
Face blank of expression.
Seeing me, people leap
To conclusions: I'm good,
Bad, better. No matter.
I snigger at flattery.
Public opinion's a prig.
But don't take it from me.
I surrender my name

And all identity. I'm nobody.
Of consequence uncertain.
I go mute. I toe the dirt.
Life goes past quietly.
      I'm boundless.

11. *Regarding progeny*

Should I give birth,
Secure humankind's place
On the earth?
All men are me,
And all women.
Why should I burden a son
To forsake all other mothers?
How cruel to saddle a daughter
With love's cost
And its promise of loss.
Love me, love me. How lonely.
Why must I birth a baby?
Why must a bloodline cage me?
I belong to no territory. I resolve to rove.
      I'm boundless.

12. *Lost*

I lost myself on an unnamed day.
I was stumped, hunting myself down
And turning up only remnants: dusty books,
Their revelations rancid, love letters
On yellowed paper. I got close many times,
But my tracks were faint, crisscrossed
By countless others.
My breath was everywhere.
But I was nowhere.

I got so tired I couldn't lift my feet,
Had to lie beneath the sky
Until I was drained of memory.
Then I felt it. Me.
The earth gave. The sky
Poured through me.
I encompassed eternity.
　　　I'm boundless.

Written October 11–13, 1986
Beida Writers' Group

BLACK HAIR

Black hair like youth
Runs wild in March.
Dark papery leaves fly
Teeming, swarming,
Bum-rushing March.

Black hair in March
Is gentle, strangers' eyes
Softer. Memory:
A feast on offer. Youth,
Born of the primordial sea—
Embrace me. Drape my skin
Old as clouds
In something suppler.

Black hair
Blown free, rootless,
Wanders the desert's
Countless tombs, sways
Across a vacant sky,
Whips at fresh mud in rain.
Days blaze past. I have
Lost sight of my own black hair
In the mirror. Let me
Watch it now
For the next thousand years.

Black hair weedy
In dirt-poor soil.
Thirsty, deluded,
Squandering its spoils.
Black hair has no idea.

The story of black hair
Is my story.
When I die, let me drift
Like a dandelion
Of black hair.

Black hair
Like holy water.
No way, there is no way
To be saved except to die.
When black hair cries,
Its tears snuff themselves out
Like candles.
So will my life cease to flicker.

Black hair
Exhausted brush fire
Fanned by misery
Whistling
Through the last century.

Black hair,
Shredded black flag
Of a woman's glory,
Ragged and battered
In March wind.
Forsaking dignity
Absolved of chastity
With its pride in knots
Black hair smiles easily
In March.

If waterfall, it will plummet.
If cloud, it will scatter.

Eyes plaintive, wide,
Black hair waits to be spun
By hardened hands
Into rock.

                              March 25, 1987

RED WALL

Hot. Having burned me but also
Warmed me. I regard it from a distance.
The flowers choking it, bleeding onto it,
Red legacy binding our generations.
From below, we thousands cast upon it a
beatific, benighted, complacent, complicit,
decorous, disconsolate, distracted, expectant,
execrative, filthy, grievous, guileless,
hallowed, hotheaded, hungry, incredulous,
indifferent, inscrutable, insubordinate, joyful,
loath, mild, peace-loving, profane, proud,
rageful, rancorous, rapt, skeptical, terrified,
tranquil, unperturbed, unrepentant,
warring eye.

October 31, 1987

NIGHTMARE

I'm bound to a stake
Planted in a nameless square.
Twigs pant at my feet
Awaiting the match.

Michael Servetus, scraggy
Madman, should be bound, too,
And hoarse from shouting.
I'm weak. I quake with rage.

With what words will the world
Be quenched? Michael Servetus
Calls on God, but I'm godless. I say,
Soon, the language of reality will be silence.

What sparks true today, blinds tomorrow.
Today, I die for a crime. Tomorrow,
People will be crowned for it.
My name will grow wide like a tree.

Flames growl and pounce.
I am consumed with fear.
Michael Servetus and I cry out
Together: *No! No!* This morning

I woke with those words
Burning my lips.

November 30, 1987

FLESH

I'm a deep cave
Starved for your wild blaze.
A daylit cloud spread above your lowlands.
My legs are nimble as a climbing vine.
My breasts, as lucent as lilies.
The breeze off a billowing Osmanthus is my face,
My dark hair rippling.
The dew from my eyes
Drenches your desperation.
The sea is bounded in its passion,
But I am boundless,
Stretching in every direction. Nowhere
Will you find flesh more spotless than mine—
Flesh to make you rich—
Flesh you alone may squander.
Peerless, my skin. Incorruptible.
Flowering again
While all around me age after age falls to ruin.

December 2, 1987

AS CLEAR AND THUS AS VIRTUOUS AS GLASS

I am as clear and thus as virtuous as glass.
To see through me, you need only glance.
Smash me to shards with the rap of a fist.
But to reach me, to really enter in,
You must travel an unfathomable distance.

December 5, 1987

THE NUDE

My eye laps at you in lamplight
Like a white-hot tongue. Longing

Draws back, then rises, tidal.

The curtain of my hair
Announces my breasts. Your lips:

A languid breeze. Like a miracle
We feast and feast and nothing is spent.

Let flesh attend to flesh, sex to sex.
O dexterous gold watch of the universe

On which one minute can straddle
A hundred years.

July 14, 1988

PRESERVED FLOWER

You must come to see me walk on fire
You must come to see me that way

You must come to see me unfasten my hair
You must come to see the old songs dancing on my lips

You must see me through the peonies
You must part the gray dusk to see me

The sight of me will outlast every other woman you see
You'll see me even after death

You need to see me broken
And, if it's not too much, also at ease

You will surely see me in this poem
See—see—see—

Darling, like a flower
That refuses to wilt

October 5, 1988

WITH WHITMAN

With you, I'm freedom itself.
Crossing the sea, traipsing woods, striding
A sunlit pasture. Good
For all manner of rough work.

Watching you
Is as natural as watching myself.
Your brow, your strong toes
As absorbing as my own.

You and I, with the jeering men and pimpled women,
With the miserable, the broken and ashamed.
You and I will sleep until dawn under one blanket.

You bring in a handful of grass,
Saying: This is truth.
I bring in an armful of winter jasmine,
Saying: This is truth.
Wind eddying in from the sea is truth.
The nibbling hare is truth.
The urge of a body in health is truth.
The bitterest and most galling notion,
Like the coarsest instinct, is truth.
I am truth.

Walt Whitman,
Wherever the grass you loved grows
There can be no lack.

Walt Whitman,
Of all things on earth that will one day decay
You will be the very last.

October 6, 1988

GLORIOUS GOLDEN BIRDS ARE SINGING

Glorious golden birds are singing
By night's bright hour
In the dark of day
Round a bonfire
Hundreds of miles away.

Love, why should I curse you still?
Happiness would only shatter me.
Already that deathless metal whirring has me
Heady and helium high,
Howling from my heart's balcony.

Glorious golden birds are singing
In the long kempt hair of morning
From the roof of a sun-ravaged cabin.
I'm not wary of scrutiny.
Yes, I'm still keen to be married.
The priest's voice whispers through the church.
I answer: *no, no*
Neither quite crying nor speaking.

Glorious golden birds are singing
In heavy hexagonal snow.
Gold, brass, bronze, zinc, copper and tin. All are my kin.
In concert, we listen. Listening,
My heart loses insistence.
This song—is it a drug? Tell me, Love:
How have I come to this lonesome world
Where nothing will accept my devotion?

February 20, 1990

SUMMER

1.

I died in summer, and to summer I've returned.
The voice of the earth
Presses into everything.
Birdsong, every birdsong, burrows
Into rock. Feathers waft and fall
Like diaphanous dresses. Rivers brim
With totems. Living waters rise and flow.
The sole singer hides in plain view.

I waited day and night for summer
To gather me in its net. Waited
For my wrongs to be sloughed away.
One night, in a storm, I swallowed
Thunderbolts and fallen flowers.
Now my soul is broken but fragrant.
Nobly, I proceed,
My bright hair overgrown as weeds.

Summer is threadbare.
My voice carries far.
Ancient rock harbors echoes
It longs to surrender,
To see plundered.
Ancient rock, still molten at the core,
Takes root in earth. My heart
Hesitates like floodwater.

2.

I've returned to summer after a long ramble.
Forest leaves mingle

Into one green bouquet.
I hover in your days
Like an old familiar haze.
Bright bars of sunlight
Break through. Softer,
The body is softer in sunlight,
Like wax that will melt
At your touch.
From the ground I look up
At unobstructed sky.
Skirts float by. I breathe
And float in thin air.
All is clear. Silence
Sings me to sleep.

I sit, at ease in summer.
You arrive on a clap of thunder.
I climb up through a vanilla orchid vine.
Your voice, quick,
Floods me. I smile.
Your beauty eclipses the moon,
Embarrasses the forest flowers.
When I think of growing old,
Fingers bowed like rickety boats,
Fear flickers in my throat.
Like a nightbird, I call and call.
My song is cold and won't be caught.
I'm keen. No matter
Where you go, a part of me follows.
Show me a road that doesn't bear
Some trace of me.

Summer brushed the hair back from my eyes.
Came, went, circled back.
My love for you is grounded,

Astonishing as stone.
You're my wild fruit.
I'm your wild fruit.
I bite into you gently, tasting.
Your flesh springs back, unbothered.
I'm the mite on a bird, a wee bat.
You're mighty. The thing of things.

3.

Oh, but the summer stretches on.
Candle flames winnow, like little lives.
Sun, moon and stars pass their moment in the sky.

I busy my hands collecting sunlight.
I breathe in the day's bright remains.
Petals fall one by one, or emigrate
On an evening breeze. Green
Is everywhere. How lonely the color.
Death's bedfellow, green arrives
Windswept and tall.

Whitman's grass covers the hills.
The wings of poets
Graze past. Starlight
Flickers with meaning, carries
All manner of secrets.
I lie down in a patch of lavender
Braced for bad news.

In the pitch of night, I sit. No reason.
Like hair, I've been handled and handled.
Now, my lover's hand guards a distance.
Young apples cling to the bough.

Thoughts catch me and don't let go.
While I watch, the sky deepens to rose.

4.

O Summer! I'm a bride behind a veil.
Whether I smile, whether I cry
A warm wind bats at the windows.
Your hunger tips me into laughter.
I'm drunk on ordinary footsteps.
Simple desire is the prize of wisdom.

I stand in the splendor of a flowering forest.
Bright flowers firm and straight,
Like girls in their first day of womanhood.
What you want to taste
You taste.
At the height of night,
Tall black ghosts examine me.
I scream, I thrash and flail.
Night pains me.
Lit windows are cool and pale.

My deepest worries root in soil.
Joy swirls in the distance like a restless ghost.
Longing is a climbing green vine.
Fear rises and falls in the dry well.
Cicada song, wanton, approaches.
My heart has been razed to the ground.
A fragrant wind blows out from everything.

Enter my empty arms.
Fill my swollen eyes.
When you pain me,
Clouds brim with gloom.

Already flowers bloom, leaves bask in bright sun.
But I'm surrounded by a chorus of my enemies.
I've spent my whole life shining for others.
You alone bask in your own light.

5.

I died in summer and to summer I return.
From the north wafts the scent of raspberry blossoms.
A golden bell tolls. Over and over.
Doors and windows thrown open
To let in the music. Something in everyone echoes.

Day after day
A white flame wanders the sky.
When cold winds blow in
Black peonies burst into shadow.
We watch as summer's green wanes,
Watch it pale to the color of water
          Flowing.
The river's far-off source is like Heaven.
Bathe in it once
And you'll understand all rivers.
Moonlight baptized in water
Enters my body.
My flesh is pure,
A cold clear trickle off the mountain spring.
Because I possess nothing
There is nothing I do not contain.

I walk the barren wilderness
Where flame has glinted and danced.
I pass heaps of fallen leaves.
I pass from flesh to ash.
My brittle heart gleams.

Far off, out beyond the visible,
I listen to the melting of ice and snow.
I lay myself upon the waters.
I glow. Virginal, absolved.

6.

Summer wears down by the day.
Is summer dying?
I sit in summer's passing, taking root.
Will I rise and leave when summer goes?
Summer, Undying Summer—
Summer entwined with snakes
Summer overgrown with roses
Summer of every face unfurled into foliage
Summer of hair grown into grass
Summer furious with prayer
Summer of zealous ghosts
Wakeful summer
Summer of life and death entwined
Weightless summer
Summer heavy as Mount Tai
Summer of naked splendor
Summer of abiding commitment
Summer of my eternal summer
Let summer devour me bit by bit
Let the body I escape
Decay in summer.

August 1990

FLAME IN THE CLOUD AT MIDNIGHT

Flame in the cloud at midnight
Blankets my bed with light.
The scent of winter jasmine
Rises from a tomb to meet my eyes.

I watch you as if from my girlhood.
I watch as if from death, anonymous
Beneath a dim sky, holding aloft
The burden of my body. Death,

Bloodless and unfeeling, is familiar.
But what if we could live that way, too?
At the moment, darling,
At the moment I'm a woman without lust.

Moonlight, like new snow,
Covers the hands and feet of night.
Huge strange faces
Fade from my windows and doors.

February 23, 1991

IN THE DISTANCE

Out past the horizon
And delimited by an
Unsentimental fog—

Past the farthest green grasses,
The flowers fading and blossoming,
Falls the torrent, the monsoon
In which a woman exalts, day and night,
Her face danced upon
By rainwater—

Out past distant heaven
And remotest earth
And the outer banks of the heart—

Past the curve of the horizon,
Neither hazy nor clear,
Where every night is a new celebration
To which your wise self and its foolish twin,
In a seamless incarnation,
Accompany you—

April 28, 1992

TALKING TO MYSELF

Most harrowing
Is the silent flame.

Quiet flame blazes up
Out of virginal silence.
Quiet as the north in new frost,
Red leaves blanketing the mountains.
Quiet as when we met.
Quiet as me that first year, shy from love.
Quiet as the hundred silent years after my death.

To swear by the sword—
To swear an oath by Heaven
Or upon the grave—
Is weaker than silence.

Do I really believe
The fiercest flame
Is silent?

May 17, 1992

NATURE ARIA

Autumn wind chases in
From all directions
And a thousand chaste leaves
Give way.

Living World,
Scatter in me the seeds
Of a thousand saplings.
Let grow a grassy heaven.
On my brow: a sun.
This bliss is yours
And alone it endures.
Music at midnight.
Young wine.
Lovers hand in hand
By daylight, moonlight.

Living World, carry me
In your mouth.
Slip on your frivolous shoes
And dance with me. My soul
Is the wild vine
Who alone has grasped it,
Who alone has seen through the awful plot,
Who will arrive in time to vanquish

The river already heavy with blossoms,
The moon spilling light onto packs
Of men. What is sadder than witless
Wolves, wind without borders,
Nationless birds, small gifts
Laden with love's intentions?

Fistfuls of rain fall hard, fill
My heart with mud. An old wind
May still come chasing in.
Resurrection fire. And me here
Laughing like a cloud in trousers,
Entreating the earth to bury me.

December 20, 1991

HEAVY RAIN

A woman showers in the rain—
A woman in the desert—
Fresh steam rising from her ribs.

She thinks, yes,
The beasts of the earth work in contentment.
Every tree, male or female, is delicate,
Watching at a lover's window in heavy rain.
Or else they are disconsolate giants,
Their debate having ages ago been settled.

Let the dark man leave.
Let the queen wait alone in her carriage of rain.
The eternal
Arrives when the rain
Arrives.

December 23, 1991

POSTPERPETUAL

When life ends,
Memory endures.
When memory ends,
What persists
Attests to the spirit.

February 17, 2002

MOTHER—

Mother—
You lounge on a cloud
Surrounded by God in His absence.

Mother—
I dream
You are always returning.
I wake and wait
For your steps in the hall.

Mother—
Mornings, I hear you puttering.
At night, you mutter and hum over the laundry.
The earth is still warm from you.
I see your needlework in the grasses that sway.
When you were alive, I worried your hair gray.
You cried like a little girl wanting her way.

Mother—
Losing you, my life has grown brittle.
The air has lost all its give.
Nothing surrounds me.
My hands have never been so greedy
For the warmth of your body,
Or my eyes more restless,
Scouring the crowd for your face in the sea.
God is real. The earth perceives us. Ghosts
Roam among the living, bargaining for an hour as flesh.

Mother—
You are a green leaf
Swept from the tree by unseasonable winds
To wander the heavens like a star.

I pray for a day each year when we might collide.
In still water I search for your eyes.

Mother—
How could you have lived once and not forever?
How have we not gone everywhere together?

Mother—
I see you on your cloud,
A shadow above this impossible city.
I hurl my voice at the sky—*Mother!*
And what answers back is the absence of everything
That isn't you.

May 2002

SONG FOR HEAVEN, EARTH AND HUMANKIND

Inscribed for the painting Celestial Music Floats *by Yi Lian*

Each blade of grass is a glorious eye,
Every ripe fruit a mouth.
Angels stretch out their thousand hands
And dewdrops and rain rain down.

All things ache for love.
Water and fire withstand each other.
Heaven journeys alongside Earth.
A small voice belts out the saddest song.

Year after year, flowers thrive.
Sea gives way to land, land to sea.
Humanity creates, ghosts endure.
The soul in the cloud dances quietly.

May 16, 2008
Written on the fifth day after the Sichuan earthquake

TO THE VIEWER

Written on the opening day of an exhibition of paintings by poets

1.

A new year. Prophecy, prophecy, prophecy . . .
Beyond your petty quarrels with others,
Are you willing to steal
The last coin from God's pocket?

Our own sins seldom surprise us.
We cast our billion wishes, burn candles
To the quick. But desire is a new trick,
A ride along a slick ridge in a little car
Whose brakes have long since
Given way.

2.

Whose hands scrub clean the soul?
Whose eyes cleave the future?
Whose mind fathoms God's intentions?
Whose compassion undoes affliction?

Whose?
Whose?
Who will teach us to see ourselves
In the calf as in the housefly, in the doe and her fawn?

Poet, if it would win you another year on this earth,
Could you?
Another day?

3.

A new year dawns, its answers
Sealed at the center of a bright maze.
Who will cross Hell's parlor to seize the key?
And by what light?
Is there yet light?
Patience. Please. Wait at least
Until your mother's voice can be

Deciphered in the distance
Calling you home for dinner.

January 2012

CORONATION OF THE ROSES

They outshine even truth.
Battered, imperial,
Their long train trails
The colonnade of years.
Desire is dead, long live desire.

2017

NOTES

Huangguoshu Waterfall:
Huangguoshu Waterfall, in China's Guizhou province, is one of the largest waterfalls in East Asia.

Love's Dance:
Section 9: The original version of the poem references Whitman's "I Sing the Body Electric." The translated version substitutes the line "You villain touch! what are you doing?" from Whitman's "Song of Myself."

A Single Woman's Bedroom:
Section 9: "Ah, linger on, thou art so fair!" are among Faust's final words in Goethe's *Faust*.

Besieged:
Section 8: Prince Pants and Panama Pants were a popular athletic look in 1980s China.

Nightmare:
Michael Servetus, a Spanish Renaissance humanist, was burned at the stake for heresy in Geneva in 1553.

Summer:
Section 4: "I'm surrounded by a chorus of my enemies" refers to the line in the original "Chu songs on all sides," a four-character idiom that describes being besieged by enemies.

Nature Aria:
"Small gifts / Laden with love's intentions" refers to the line in the original "goose feathers from a thousand miles away," an allusion to the great affection represented by a small gift in a Tang dynasty story.

Song for Heaven, Earth and Humankind:
"Sea gives way to land, land to sea" refers to a Chinese idiom that describes the great changes in the world brought by the passing of time.

伊蕾诗选

绿树对暴风雨的迎接

千条万条的狂莽的手臂啊，
纵然你是必给我损伤的鞭子，
我又怎能不昂首迎接你?!
    迎接你，即使遍体绿叶碎为尘泥!
    与其完好无损地困守孤寂，
    莫如绽破些伤口敞向广宇。

千声万声的急骤的嘶鸣啊，
纵然你是必给我震悚的蹄踏，
我又怎能不昂首迎接你?!
    迎接你，即使遍体绿叶碎为尘泥!
    与其枯萎时默默地飘零，
    莫如青春时轰轰烈烈地给你。

1982.7.30

黄果树大瀑布

白岩石一样砸下来
　　砸
　　下
　　来
砸碎大墙下款款的散步
砸碎"维也纳别墅"那架小床
砸碎死水河那个幽暗的夜晚
砸碎那尊白蜡的雕像
砸碎那座小岛，茅草的小岛
砸碎那段无人的走廊
砸碎古陵墓前躁动不安的欲念
砸碎重复了又重复的缠绵的失望
砸碎沙地上那株深秋的苹果树
砸碎旷野里那幅水彩画
砸碎红窗帘下那把流泪的吉他
砸碎海滩上那迷茫中短暂的彷徨
把我砸得粉碎粉碎吧
我灵魂不散
要去寻找那一片永恒的土壤
强盗一样去占领、占领
哪怕像这瀑布
千年万年被钉在
　　悬
　　崖
　　上

1985.9.20

72

陌生人之间

陌生人，谁能测出你我之间的距离？
这距离或者像欧洲和太平洋，
这距离或者只是不可再分的，
一层微薄的空间，
也许只需擦亮一根火柴，
两个陌生的世界就可以互相看见，
也许面对面一分钟，
然后就可以跨进那个并不存在的门坎，
也许当敏感的手指碰到手指，
两颗心就奏响了一曲无声的和弦，
也许当脚印重复，再重复，
寂寞的行程就会消除韧性的防线，
也许一次礼节性的谦让，
却彼此获得了索取一切的特权。
陌生人啊，当一切也许都没有发生，
你我就在交臂之间走过去了，
各走各的经过选择的道路，
直到死，我们没有一句交谈。
那两个辉煌的思想的碰撞是可能的啊！
……
然而，一切都没有发生。
因为陌生，我们不可能恨不相逢，
而这种恨几乎充满了我们每个人的生活。

1985

野餐

在滚着太阳的草坡上
我们吃五香鱼
吃你的短短的胡须

多么想让你的胡须又长又乱
像个野人
我想做一回野人

哦，吃吧，吃吧
吃古老的董酒
吃面包黄油

吃你的逃跑的手
吃你的漆黑的头发
吃你的响着笑声的牙
直到把太阳吃完

剩下满天飞流的云
我们吃不完了

1986.3.5

我的秘密

苦水捆绑了所有的经纬线
不屈者日日遭受海蚀
平凡的梦长满了青苔

如期相会恰似如期分手
却无法放弃这
残忍的剪裁

呼声被碾碎
丝丝缕缕的飘落
一次又一次
手指焚成了火
心，却来不及悲哀
（那值得恐惧的是什么呢？）

厚厚的书信也散亡了
唯有秘密的署名像野蔷薇
　　开满了窗台

1986.6.15

情舞

1. 这一天我中了巫术

这一天我中了巫术
你伸出手，我就跟了你去
跨过惊慌的灯光
我是这样光明正大地贴近了你
蓝外套一下子变成敦煌彩袖
你不可抗拒的力量使我百依百顺
我已经孤独地站立了很久
可是我曾经说过
我不会绝望
      这一次相遇照亮了历史的缺陷
      不安定因素从此诞生

2. 疯狂的探戈

疯狂的探戈平地而起
切分音把我一切为二
一半是右腿
一半是左腿
整个生存被一分为二
脚步被一分为二
对话被一分为二
经验
知觉
心曲
你也被一分为二
我痛悔这残忍的命运
幻想着回归完整
你是一体
我是一体
      不不，你我原本只是一体

被宙斯一分两半
亿万年来渴望着融合

3. 禁忌

舞曲落下一片又一片
我的渴望被层层包起
崇拜就是禁忌
我禁忌什么我自己也不知道
我无视一切
却无力推开压顶而来的天空
这一天我中了巫术
与你赤诚相见的都是假话
我毫不甘心地拒绝了你
当你悄然规避
仿佛陆地在胸前陷落
我的呼叫被回声堵塞
是无形的手铸就了我的错误
为了避免一个可怜的悲剧
我扼杀了灵魂的自由
　　让我的理智从此漆黑一片
　　我愿意被你主宰

4. 死亡如此渺小

当人们四散离座
我独自留恋红红的太阳
你把黑色的影子交给我
灵魂光芒四射
你独立着
我独立着
最大的痛苦是可望不可即
你说要看看我的眼睛
激情的寒流袭击了我

我的四面是万丈悬崖
你的话是神秘的栅栏
死亡如此渺小
　　　我确信了这个真实的时刻
　　　我要披荆斩棘开拓你
　　　在荒原写上我的名字

5. 赤裸的热情

两束目光相撞成为闪电
赤裸的热情无处躲避
我放弃所有无谓的挣扎
唯一的道路化为乌有
（我不知道向谁请教）
向左还是向右
我来不及顾念后果
向前是盲目，向后还是盲目
即使乐曲永无止境
即使它在下一秒钟立即终结
　　　你的目光使我堕入深渊
　　　我因此死而无憾

6. 我就是水

《卡普里岛》、《卡普里岛》
如水的节奏波光闪耀
我就是渔岛之女
我把自己铺在夜色里
眼泪滔滔
柔情似水横流
我的痛苦千姿百态
围绕你翩翩起舞
弹性的肌肤任凭你
任凭你蹂躏
　　　我的快感是苦难的快感

我的快感是柔弱者的快感
我的柔弱胜过刚强

7. 永远的未知

我还不谙熟你的步伐
头发却肆无忌惮地飘扬
朋友
谁能确认朋友的含义
未来世界的真理
在今天引起惊慌
我愿你只是朋友，两个月亮
一个在水
一个在天
谁能断定他们是一个还是两个
朋友永远是一个未知
即使你占有了他的全部
还有一些东西你不可能占有
你的神奇感动了我
我的幻觉永不消逝
我宁愿你不是你
不让你不像你
　　　永世的诅咒使我陷入迷恋

8. 没有心就没有圆

你是半径
我是半径
这是一颗肉体的星星
各个部位闪烁光芒
各个部位都非常美好
向心力
向心
向——心
你围绕着我之心

我围绕着你之心
没有心就没有圆
有心的圆才是真实的圆
不知是什么巫术
一个个虚假的圆也团团旋转
向我们合拢、合拢
我们被挤扁，像一张圆圆的废纸
在人海中飘零
　　　六月雪是昨天的故事
　　　从此六月再没有下雪

9. 阻力的诱惑

走向你，走向你
中间隔着永恒的距离
你的胸膛如热岛咄咄逼人
我却无力跨过这世纪的鸿沟
阻力造成了诱惑
我欲望的价值百倍地增长
我在无形的阻遏中挣扎
每一秒钟是一个挫折
现在我只剩下了一种本能
要接触你"带电的肉体"
对于陌生我不再充满敌意
　　　我从没有这样自信于我的纯洁
　　　对于你我再没有危险

10. 迪斯科之恋

你像狮像牛
我像鹿像蛇
多么想被你追逐
被你围困
天真无畏地嬉戏

喷射你久蓄的激情
如果这是那一片原野
即使只披了两片树叶
也会遭到嘲笑
文明世世代代装饰了我们
冲动被缚于山岩
噩梦中，我被雕刻出满脸花纹
银灰色的花纹中有粉红的小花成双
啊！我宁愿死
也不敢再看自己一眼
　　噩梦将使我终生心悸
　　我庆幸你是一只蓬勃的野兽

11. 我们去流浪

今夜旋律这样忧伤
走吧，我们去流浪
流浪的生活是自由的生活
流浪者的法律是自由万岁
我们被释放
思想四下逃散
没有繁文缛节
纸币当成卫生纸
所有的道路我们任意选择
在任何一块土地
让我们同行同宿
最好碰到洪水大发
或者暴徒成群
让我们的四肢发达如初
反抗的力量天翻地覆
　　流浪（星期日）
　　流浪（星期一）
　　流浪（星期二）
　　流浪（星期三）

流浪（星期四）
流浪（星期五）
流浪（星期六）

12. 天经地义的败类

我这样疲惫
心神不安
你的目光直视我
以跳荡的节奏向欲火挑衅
你迅速地侵蚀我
攫取我
我的衣饰不翼而飞
唯一的秘密暴露无遗
最可笑的废话是——
你到底要什么
无谓的牺牲已经太久了
还没有开始已将近终结
有一些伤害无法补偿
　　　最公平的是最残忍的
　　　你这样非凡的健康
　　　注定是天经地义的败类

13. 没有加冕的教徒

辉煌的钟声敲起来
我们以手相握膜拜《圣母颂》
我们是没有加冕的教徒
没有宣誓
不懂戒律
从早到晚安分守己
我所要的东西没有得到
到处都是虚伪的陷阱
我随时准备比鸿毛还轻的献身
我无法避开那个忌讳的数字

恐怖的面目时刻引诱我
我想挣脱时已被捕获
旧约书我们背了三遍
因此我们爱上耶稣
只有唯一可行的仪式
每天晚上点一盘蚊香
遗憾的是我们恨上了信奉
信奉什么就谈笑间把它砸碎
有一次我们信奉了自己
为表示自杀我们去海里洗澡
　　　童贞圣母，请不必担心
　　　我们从没有对你相信

14. 我的禁区荒芜一片

　　　我梦寐以求
让我们单独跳一段舞蹈
这里危机四伏
命里注定了这一次灾难
当你的手臂伸向我
我就完全属于了你
乳房闪着幽暗的白光
唇齿相依
你的手宽大、温暖
充当了夏娃遮体的树叶
我的禁区荒芜一片
没有过生命的体验
弱质在星星下不堪一击
呼声幽咽，痛快淋漓
所有幻觉聚成弹性的物态
所有坚实的理解溶化为液体
　　　让生命上天堂！
　　　让灵魂下地狱！

15. 白天鹅最后的歌声

点一支蜡烛
在暗淡的墙壁上
这是《婚礼进行曲》
省略了所有法律程序
进行曲是全权代表
进行曲进行就是一切进行
必要的都是绳索
今天必定成为过去
让我们提前过一天美好的明天
因为我就要衰老
最好是野餐一顿
并且，没有客人
然后
然后
啊！我感到威严的眼睛封锁了门窗
在客人的掌声中我们不能接吻
瞬间叛逆将付出重大牺牲
进行曲是白天鹅最后的歌声
　　　等待而死或者叛逆而死
　　　为什么我不能获得生存

16. 没有目的地的旅行

这一天我中了巫术
旅行的目的地被我忘记
　　　找不到
目的地是一个罪大恶极的名字
我们无法避开天罗地网
深夜亦难逃四面杀机
通往目的地没有道路
我们在距其遥远的地方徘徊
背道而驰
失去了目的

失魂落魄
我们疲劳已极
血从眼睛里流出
还需要多久、多久
目的地无法抵达
我全身正布满厚厚的皱纹
　　为什么
　　为什么
　　我这样悲伤
　　我感到一生过于漫长

1986年9月中旬

独身女人的卧室

1. 镜子的魔术

你猜我认识的是谁
她是一个，又是许多个
在各个方向突然出现
又瞬间消隐
她目光直视
没有幸福的痕迹
她自言自语，没有声音
她是立体，又是平面
她给你什么你也无法接受
她不能属于任何人
——她就是镜子中的我
整个世界除以二
剩下的一个单数
一个自由运动的独立的单子
一个具有创造力的精神实体
——她就是镜子中的我
我的木框镜子就在床头
它一天做一百次这样的魔术
　　　你不来与我同居

2. 土耳其浴室

这小屋裸体的素描太多
一个男同胞偶然推门
高叫"土耳其浴室"
他不知道在夏天我紧锁房门
我是这浴室名副其实的顾客
顾影自怜——
四肢很长，身材窈窕
臀部紧凑，肩膀斜削
碗状的乳房轻轻颤动

每一块肌肉都充满激情
我是我自己的模特
我创造了艺术，艺术创造了我
床上堆满了画册
袜子和短裤在桌子上
玻璃瓶里迎春花枯萎了
地上乱开着暗淡的金黄
软垫和靠背四面都是
每个角落都可以安然入睡
　　　你不来与我同居

3. 窗帘的秘密

白天我总是拉着窗帘
以便想象阳光下的罪恶
或者进入感情王国
心理空前安全
心理空前自由
然后幽灵一样的灵感纷纷出笼
我结交他们达到快感高潮
新生儿立即出世
智力空前良好
如果需要幸福我就拉上窗帘
痛苦立即变成享受
如果我想自杀我就拉上窗帘
生存欲望油然而生
拉上窗帘听一段交响曲
爱情就充满各个角落
　　　你不来与我同居

4. 自画像

所有的照片都把我丑化
我在自画像上表达理想
我把十二种油彩合在一起

我给它起名叫 P 色
我最喜欢神秘的头发
蓬松的刘海像我侄女
整个脸部我只画了眉毛
敬祝我像眉毛一辈子长不大
眉毛真伟大充满了哲学
既不认为是，也不认为非
既不光荣，也不可耻
既不贞洁，也不淫秽
既不是生，也不是死
我把自画像挂在低矮的墙壁
每日朝见这唯一偶像
　　　你不来与我同居

5. 小小聚会

小小餐桌铺一块彩色台布
迷离的灯光泄在模糊的头顶
喝一口红红的酒
我和几位老兄起来跳舞
像舞厅的少男少女一样
我们不微笑，沉默着
显得昏昏欲醉
独身女人的时间像一块猪排
你却不来分食
我在偷偷念一个咒语——
让我的高跟鞋跳掉后跟
噢！这个世界已不是我的
我好像出生了一个世纪
面容腐朽，脚上也长了皱纹
独身女人没有好名声
只是因为她不再年轻
　　　你不来与我同居

6. 一封请柬

一封请柬使我如释重负
坐在藤椅上我若有所失
曾为了他那篇论文我同意约会
我们是知音，知音，只是知音
为什么他不问我点儿什么
每次他大谈现代派、黑色幽默
可他一点也不学以致用
他才思敏捷，卓有见识
可他毕竟是孩子
他温柔多情，单纯可爱
他只能是孩子
他文雅庄重，彬彬有礼
他永远是孩子，是孩子
——我不能证明自己是女人
这一次婚礼是否具有转折意义
人是否可以自救或者互救
　　　你不来与我同居

7. 星期日独唱

星期日没有人陪我去野游
公园最可怕，我不敢问津
我翻出现存的全体歌本
在土耳其浴室里流浪
从早饭后唱到黄昏
头发唱成 1
眼睛唱成 2
耳朵唱成 3
鼻子唱成 4
脸蛋唱成 5
嘴巴唱成 6
全身上下唱成 7
表哥的名言万岁——

歌声是心灵的呻吟
音乐使痛苦可以忍受
孤独是伟大的
　（我不要伟大）
疲乏的眼睛憩息在四壁
头发在屋顶下飞像黑色蝙蝠
　　　你不来与我同居

8: 哲学讨论

我朗读唯物主义哲学——
物质第一
我不创造任何物质
这个世界谁需要我
我甚至不生孩子
不承担人类最基本的责任
在一堆破烂的稿纸旁
讨论艺术讨论哲学
第一，存在主义
第二，达达主义
第三，实证主义
第四，超现实主义
终于发现了人类的秘密
为活着而活着
活着有没有意义
什么是最高意义
我有无用之用
我的气息无所不在
我决心进行无意义结婚
　　　你不来与我同居

9. 暴雨之夜

暴雨像男子汉给大地以鞭楚
躁动不安瞬间缓解为深刻的安宁

六种欲望掺和在一起
此刻我什么都要什么都不要
暴雨封锁了所有的道路
走投无路多么幸福
我放弃了一切苟且的计划
生命放任自流
暴雨使生物钟短暂停止
哦，暂停的快乐深奥无边
　　"请停留一下"
我宁愿倒地而死
　　你不来与我同居

10. 象征之梦

我一人占有这四面墙壁
我变成了枯燥的长方形
我做了一个长方形的梦
长方形的天空变成了狮子星座
一会儿头部闪闪发亮
一会儿尾部闪闪发亮
突然它变成一匹无缰的野马
向无边的宇宙飞驰而去
套马索无力地转了一圈垂落下来
宇宙漆黑没有道路
每一步都有如万丈深渊
自由的灵魂不知去向
也许她在某一天夭折
　　你不来与我同居

11. 生日蜡烛

生日蜡烛像一堆星星
方方的屋顶是闭锁的太阳系
空间无边无沿
宇宙无意中创造了人

我们的出生纯属偶然
生命应当珍惜还是应当挥霍
应当约束还是应当放任
上帝命令：生日快乐
所有举杯者共同大笑
迎接又临近一年的死亡
因为是全体人的恐惧
所以全体人都不恐惧
可惜青春比蜡烛还短
火焰就要熄灭
这是我一个人的痛苦
　　　你不来与我同居

12. 女士香烟

我吸它是因为它细得可爱
点燃我做女人的欲望
我欣赏我吸烟的姿势
具有一种世界性美感
烟雾造成混沌的状态
寂寞变得很甜蜜
我把这张报纸翻了一翻
戒烟运动正在广泛开展
并且得到了广泛支持
支持的并不身体力行
不支持的更不为它作出牺牲
谁能比较出吸烟的功德与危害
戒烟和吸烟只好并行
各取所需
是谁制定了不可戒的戒律
高等人因此而更加神奇
低等人因此而成为罪犯
今夜我想无罪而犯
　　　你不来与我同居

13. 想

我把剩余时间通通用来想
我赋予想一个形式：室内散步
我把体验过的加以深化
我把未得到的改为得到
我把发生过的加以进展
我把未曾有的化成幻觉
不能做的都想
怯于对你说的都想
法律踟蹰在地下
眼睁睁仰望着想
罗网和箭矢失去了目标
任凭想胡作非为
我想签证去想的王国居住
我只担心那里已经人口泛滥
　　你不来与我同居

14. 绝望的希望

这繁华的城市如此空旷
小小的房子目标暴露
白天黑夜都有监护人
我独往独来，充满恐惧
我不可能健康无损
众多的目光如刺我鲜血淋漓
我祈祷上帝把那一半没有眼的椰子
　　分给全体公民
道路已被无形的障碍封锁
我怀着绝望的希望夜夜等你
你来了会发生世界大战吗
你来了黄河会决口吗
你来了会有坏天气吗
你来了会影响收麦子吗

面对所恨的一切我无能为力
我最恨的是我自己
　　你不来与我同居

1986年9月末

被围困者

1. 主体意识

我被围困
就要疯狂地死去

2. 我要到哪里去

这是一次逃亡者的旅行
走下火车我茫然四顾
我要到哪里去？
陌生的街道不宽不窄
路面枯燥无味
路的名字似乎很有来历
而我从哪里来？
那个熟悉的城市曾经没有我
我从哪里来？
我为什么而来？
有一个莫名其妙的目的
一个目的是一个死亡
最终目的是最终死亡
怎能让目的把我分段消灭
我要无目的地走下去
我突然仰面凝视滚动的乌云
啊！这是一个凶恶的无底深渊
三秒钟后我心惊胆战闭上了眼睛
无底！无底！
宇宙无限大，没有边沿
没有边沿以外是什么？
愚蠢透顶，没有边沿哪有以外
真是不可思议
没有边沿这个形象够我想象一万年
我的思维因此而无边无际
我的精神因此而无边无际
　　我无边无沿

3. 我是谁

在温暖的草地上打开化妆盒
在约会前我再一次会见自己
为了接近国际标准
我开始大胆地修改鄙人
眉毛加长
眼睛加大
睫毛加黑
嘴唇加红
我是谁?
现在我又是谁?
光荣与羞耻属于这张脸会怎样?
属于另一张脸又会怎样?
我在为谁恪守戒律?
我是谁?
我的朋友,你为什么还不来
来看看我现在是谁
我将变成谁
情欲的洪水漫过了围墙
　　　我无边无沿

4. 我不明白我自己

你要把我画成什么颜色?
黄皮肤吗?不,绝不
你不知道我的气息的颜色
我的感情的颜色你也不清楚
还有我的观念
我的幻觉
我的罪恶的心理
你都看不见
你看不见我的颜色
我也看不见我的颜色
我希望我是绿色

像鬼的颜色
而鬼果真是绿色的吗？
我希望我是白色
像天使的颜色
而天使果真是白色的吗？
无论恐惧的和崇拜的我都不太了解
我为什么要恐惧和崇拜呢？
我真不明白我自己
我永远也不会完全了解我自己
　　我无边无沿

5. 被缚的苦恼

案头书是一本历史悠久的典籍
我每日有两小时伏案攻读
这白色的长方形渐渐扩大
终于把我整个框在其中
长方形真是魔力无边
我站起它就变得长些
我坐下它就变得短些
任我变动
它紧紧随形
我的脚迈不出它的门槛
它跟随我到任何一个地方
任何时候与我同在
被缚的苦恼不如死
我在偷偷积蓄经验
酝酿一次爆炸行动
　　我无边无沿

6. 墙外是谁

五面墙壁切断了我的日光
肉体与天空隔离
我在室内安然洗澡

瞬间后感觉我是身处地狱
我迫不及待要冲出去
墙外是谁？
谁在墙外？
是谁？
墙外是谁？
我迫不及待要冲出去
我宁愿满身灰尘
是泥土做成
我不需要墙壁
那墙，一分钟也不要存在
　　我无边无沿

7. 堕入黑暗世界

客厅糊满高贵的壁纸
你的语言像钟声回荡
这金属的声音把我包围
所有的道路隐而不见
我试图冲破这声音
却把它撞得更响
我只有飞快地书写笔记
那黑暗的字迹又把我包围
我堕入了黑暗世界
像瞎子寸步难行
你能否把我们已知的另做讲解？
你能否将你认为正确的给予否定？
愿你的语言是白纸，薄薄的
最好千疮百孔
　　我无边无沿

8. 巴拿马封锁线

黄昏我逛服装自由市场
王子裤、东芝鞋、新潮鞋

这里简直是新名词发明处
我试身巴拿马裤顿时高度兴奋
双腿紧绷绷优美的曲线暴露
巴拿马把我的肌肉围困
我的步态立即向巴拿马投降
我要极力像一个巴拿马
巴拿马是什么东西？
为什么我要像一个巴拿马
巴拿马有道貌岸然的边沿
苛刻的边沿
蛮横的边沿
我能否走到边沿以外呢？
我能否在我愿意的任何时候
走到边沿以外呢？
　　我无边无沿

9. 一个金字塔

我回到家时已是月照小窗
家人们正襟危坐在餐桌边等候
我们分三面恭敬地坐好
一个金三角
一个金字塔
这古老的建筑光照世界
巨大、坚固、不可摧毁
谁也不知道它固守的秘密
它只沉默着，沉默
金字塔为什么不是一面或者几面
究竟谁应该光荣牺牲？
这禁锢的岁月还要多久
我已四肢僵硬
热血停止流动
这伟大的名誉我再也背负不动
我宁愿一朝毁灭
堕落成历史罪人

我只要呼吸，只要呼吸
　　我无边无沿

10. 我的意义不确定

我在大庭广众下诉说秘密
毫无表情
人们从一百种角度观察我
得出一百种结论
我比你想象的还要好
你渺小的奉承让我发笑
我比你想象的还要坏
我知道你绝不会恐惧
因为任何人和我一样坏
舆论是个虚伪的家伙
我蔑视它，使它无地自容
我本来是不确定的
我的意义也不确定
知道我的名字的都想鉴定我
我因此失去了对话
我孤独地坐在沙土地上
生命默默地流逝
　　我无边无沿

11. 生孩子问题

我是否要生一个孩子？
人类因我而延续
所有的男人都是我
所有的女人都是我
为什么我要再生一个孩子？
让他只认我一人为母亲
多么残酷
我擅自付出代价
债务却要孩子还清

让孩子认我，爱我，依恋我
注定有一天他会突然寂寞
为什么我要再生一个孩子？
建起这血统的牢笼
我不属于任何一块领地
我要走遍天下
　　我无边无沿

12. 我把我丢失了

不知是哪一天我把我丢失了
我惊慌失措，全副武装去找我
到处都是我的弃物
诗集生了锈
道德已经腐烂
情书萎缩
还有许多意外收获
只是没有脚印
老朽的和新鲜的道路纵横交错
到处都是我的气息
到处没有我
我精疲力竭再也抬不起双脚
终于倒在天空下
忘掉了一切
哦，我突然感觉到了我
我在大地上嘣嘣跳动
我的形态和天空合为一体
我包罗万象无所不有
　　我无边无沿

1986.10.11～13
北大作家班

黑头发

黑头发
青春的痕迹
在三月里奔跑
黑色的脆弱的叶子满天飘零
纷纷扬扬
铺满了三月

黑头发
在三月里温柔千倍
那些凋落的目光辉煌灿烂
记忆是如画的晚餐
妙龄时期在三月里复苏
走出没有性别的深渊
用柔韧的长丝包裹我吧
皮肤已苍老如云

黑头发
在沙漠与荒冢流离失所
在晴朗的天空风尘遮面
在雨中践踏泥泞
在火红的日子里黯然失色
我没有在镜中好好看过
我的黑头发
我想从此看上一千年

黑头发
蓬勃的野草
在卑贱的土壤里痛饮
摇摇摆摆
疯狂地生长着幻想

在破灭的日子里破灭
黑头发，并不知道

黑头发的经历
是我的经历
让我在这一刻死去吧
从此，从此，秀发如云

黑头发
流水一样
无法，无法！无法……挽留
就要沦丧

黑头发
火烛一样
就要流干眼泪
从此用什么照耀我的生活

黑头发
疲惫的野火
在最后的时光里凄艳地嚎叫

黑头发
黑色的柔软的旗帜
一个女性最后的骄傲
在三月的风中
千疮百孔
是的，她背叛了尊严的血统
没有贞洁的光芒
最后的骄傲，在三月里
自由地微笑

是瀑布，就要流淌尽了
是乌云，就要散去了
黑头发张大惊恐的眼睛
乞望的眼睛
等待着在你男性的手中
结为岩石

1987.3.25

红墙

火一样
焚烧了我又使我温暖
我远远地瞧着它
那些鲜花，曾潮水般把它淹没
又在它上面溅满热血
红色的高贵的血统
光荣世代相传
成千上万的卑贱者向它投去信仰的
怀疑的、热爱的、憎恶的、尊重的
轻蔑的、关怀的、冷漠的、亲近的
陌生的、祝福的、诅咒的、期待的
绝望的、渴盼的、灰心的、狂热的
死寂的、镇定的、惶恐的、忧郁的
开朗的、悲哀的、快乐的、不幸的
幸福的、沮丧的、得意的、自卑的
骄傲的、痛苦的、欢乐的、文雅的
粗鲁的、正经的、淫亵的、痴呆的
狡黠的、阴险的、敦厚的、和平的
挑战的、友好的、仇恨的、温和的
凶恶的目光

                                    1987.10.31

噩梦

我被绑在火刑柱上
火刑柱设在一个现代的广场
四面干柴伸出愚蠢的舌头
准备着那噬血的一刻

塞维特斯这个瘦弱的狂人
竟和我绑在一起
他声嘶力竭地大声咒骂
而我因过度的愤怒而周身无力

该有什么话要对这个世界说呢？
塞维特斯在呼唤上帝
可是我没有上帝，我说：
"未来面对现实只好沉默"

今天的真理要在明天发光
今天我以这个罪名死去了
明天人们会因这个罪名获得光荣
我的名字将因我可怕的命运而不朽

刑场的大火从四面烧起来了
我的平凡的肉体惊恐万状
塞维特斯和我一起大喊着：不！不！
我就这样大喊着从噩梦中醒来

1987.11.30

我的肉体

我是深深的岩洞
渴望你野性之光的照射
我是浅色的云
铺满你僵硬的陆地
双腿野藤一样缠绕
乳房百合一样透明
脸盘儿桂花般清香
头发的深色枝条悠然荡漾
我的眼睛饱含露水
打湿了你的寂寞
大海的激情是有边沿的
而我没有边沿
走遍世界
你再也找不到比我更纯洁的肉体
我的肉体，给你财富
又让你挥霍
我的长满青苔的皮肤足可抵御风暴
在废墟中永开不败

1987.12.2

玻璃一样晶莹而高贵的

玻璃一样晶莹而高贵的那是我
看穿我只需要凝眸一瞬
打碎我只需要弹指一挥
可是要到达我的身边
需经过意想不到的距离

1987.12.5

裸体

我的目光在灯光下，
像白色的舌头在你的肌肉上跳跃
热烈地吃着一顿美餐

我的情欲在涨潮
薄薄的墙壁一寸一寸后退
长发在乳房上挂起秀帘
你的嘴唇像阵阵微风来袭

我们始终没有丢掉
那颗神秘的果子
彼此不知羞耻

肉体吮吸肉体死而又生
宇宙柔软的金表啊
一分钟就是一百年

1988.7.14

不谢的花

你要踏着红红的火焰来看我
你要这样来看我

你要循着温柔的青丝来看我
你要含着那首民歌来看我

透过密密的蔷薇花你看我
撩起灰色的黄昏你看我

看过了所有的女人你再看我
看到了死亡你再看我

绝望的时候你一定要看我
漫不经心的时候请看看我

读着我的这篇诗歌你看我
看我，看我，看我

亲爱的，你的
不谢的花

1988.10.5

110

和惠特曼在一起

和你在一起
我自己就是自由!
穿过海洋，走过森林，跨过牧场
我会干各种粗活

看着你
像看我自己那样亲近而着迷
你的额头，你的健壮的脚趾
如同我的一样美丽

我和你，和陌生的男人女人们在一起
和不幸的、下贱的、羞耻的人们在一起
在一个被单下睡到天明

你捧来一把草叶
你说：这就是真理
我抱来一丛迎春
我说：这就是真理
从海上吹来的风是真理
一只小兔子的咀嚼是真理
一个健康人的欲望是真理
那些最隐秘的，最难堪的念头是真理
一个文盲所知道的一切常识是真理
我就是真理

惠特曼
你的草叶在哪里生长
哪里就不会有真理的荒凉

惠特曼
如果地球上所有的东西都会腐朽
你是最后腐朽的一个

1988.10.6

辉煌的金鸟在叫

辉煌的金鸟在叫
在夜的白昼
在白昼的夜
在大火之上
在千里之遥

爱人，为什么我要诅咒你
我已不能忍受幸福
这不朽的金属之声敲击我
已灌满了空气
在我心的平台上疯狂地演唱

辉煌的金鸟在叫
在清晨梳理的长发里
在那座灰砖的小屋顶上
我检查身体时竟没有受到侮辱
是的，我很想结婚
教堂里牧师的声音也很温和
我说：不，不
如泣如诉

辉煌的金鸟在叫
在六角形的大雪里
六种金属和我血肉相连
和我一起倾听
我失去了爱情的折磨
为不朽的声音所陶醉
爱人，我已坠入这寂寥的世界
不能作任何献身

1990.2.20

112

夏

一

我在夏天死又回到夏天
天——籁——之——声
从四野落下
有无数鸟鸣嵌进坚硬的石头
羽毛零落为处女华裳
河流中藏满鱼的图腾
大水为瀑发出空洞的轰响
唯一的、唯一的歌手
隐蔽于不为人知的地方

我日夜等待的夏
占有了我
像网中的游鱼
无望中等待着刑罚锐减
在大雨的夜晚
我痛饮雷霆和落英
灵魂破碎而芳香
坦坦荡荡地走
灿烂的秀发疯长

夏
透明得千疮百孔
这时候我的话传得很远
岩石上充满了回声
渴望四面受敌
渴望献身
灼热的果核落地生根
心如大水彷徨

二

我远途跋涉回到夏天
树叶与树叶
生息在彼此的气味里
我生息在你的日子里
暴躁又安详
在无休无止的阴霾中
种植着尖锐的阳光
身体在阳光里变软、变软
一触即化
在没有墙的大地
看裙裾在空中飘过
我在空中飘过
我呼吸着狭窄的空气
丢掉幻想
准备无歌而眠

我坐在夏天，心安理得
你被雷雨声带来
我被香草籽带来
你的轻捷的叫声
让我微笑
我对你的想象
闭月羞花
当我想到安逸的晚年
手指就像弯弯的小船
我的恐惧是顽皮的夜莺
时隐时现捉不住
歌声冰凉
我是如此热烈的女人
无论你走多远
我的指纹足可把道路铺满

夏天，在我发鬓隆隆地走过
又返回

我对你的情爱席地而坐
朴素又漂亮
你是我的野果
我是你的野果
你我轻轻咬上一口
又在瞬间复原
我对于你是弱小的一物
你对于我是物中之物

三

而夏在漫长地延伸
生命的烛火低声合唱着
这时天上有日月星辰

我把阳光一把一把地捧下来
在辉煌的残骸中静静地喘息
花瓣一片一片落地或者远走
在有风的晚上
接天连地的绿色有多么孤独啊
它从死那边来
个个独立无援

惠特曼的草叶遍布山冈
诗人的翅膀
伸手可及
星星们举火为号
告诉我不为人知的秘密
我以蓑衣草为紧邻
守候着恶劣的消息

在这黑夜，我无端地坐着
像头发，承受沉重的抚摸
恋人的手指停在距我很近的地方
苹果还未成熟

它强迫我日夜分神
注视它慢慢变红的青色

四

夏啊夏，落下了红红的盖头
我哭泣或者笑都是新娘
暖风天真无邪地咬着窗户
你的贪婪让我哑然失笑
只是寻常的脚步就醉倒了我
素日的欲望是灿烂的珍宝

我在西黄莲的光辉中站立
鲜艳，饱满，少女一样
你要品尝
你就品尝
当暗夜围困了我
黑黑的高高的鬼就俯身向我
我尖叫着，扑打着翅膀
黑夜好疼啊
窗户也脸色蜡黄

我的深愁落地生根
看欢乐游来游去，幽灵一样
思念葱葱茏茏，攀缘而来
恐惧在枯井里升升降降
有蝉声袭来
我的心潮被夷为平地
白云和皮肤一起飘出芳香

到我空空的手臂中来
到我呻吟的眼中来
当我恨你
云就变得潮湿无比
花已开，叶已盛

四面楚歌如墙
照耀我的一生一世
只需你把身体点亮

五

我在夏天死又回到夏天
北方传来红莓花的清香
金黄的钟声接连地响
轻易地推开门窗
让从古至今的音乐浅浅荡漾

日复一日
白色的火焰在天空流浪
当凉风吹来
黑色的牡丹投下阴影
我们守候着绿色的木栅
在大雨中看它变成柔软的水
　　流淌
远方来的河流就像天堂
你只进入一次
就领略了所有的河流
坚强的月光浸入水中
成为我身体的部分
肉体是如此清澈见底
是山泉，可分成点点滴滴
因为我一无所有
所以我包罗万象

我在荒凉的野外行走
在穿过落叶的时候
烧成四肢舞蹈的篝火
当我化成纯洁的灰烬
干燥的心闪闪发光

甚至在极目不到的远方
我听到冰消雪化
我在所有的水中照耀我
成为举世单纯的一物

六

夏天在日日销蚀
夏天就要死了么？
我坐在夏天里日日生根
我要随夏天去了么？
噢，你不朽的夏天
被蛇紧紧缠绕的夏天
鲜花遍体的夏天
耳朵，嘴唇，眼睛长成叶子的夏天
头发长成青草的夏天
人子热烈的祈祷夏天
如火如荼的灵魂夏天
永不安眠的夏天
生死相连的夏天
轻如鸿毛的夏天
重如泰山的夏天
赤裸如初、壮美如初的夏天
矢志不移，终生不渝的夏天
我永生的恋人夏天
我在夏天重生重死
让夏天一口一口把我吞食吧
让我残破的肢体
腐烂在夏天

1990.8

夜半云中的火焰

夜半云中的火焰
把光芒铺满我的睡床
远处开迎春花的坟
在我眼中散发奇香

如少女时看你
如无名的死魂
在暗淡的天空下
孤独地高举着头颅

我们习惯了这样死
现在我们要习惯这样生
这时，亲爱的
这时我是无欲的女人

枯萎的月光雪一样温柔
盖住夜的手脚
几个巨大而陌生的面孔
消失在四面门窗

1991.2.23

远方

远在天涯
用锋利的雾
切断柔肠

天涯，芳草
花谢，花发
该怎样忘却雕刻的容颜啊
热爱大雨的女人
日日，夜夜
雨水洗面

天，这样远
地，这样远
心啊，这样远

远在天涯
未曾秽，未曾净
夜夜是佳期
有一个大智大愚的你
十全十美的你
陪伴你

1992.4.28

自语

最炽烈最痛心的是
静静的火焰

静静的火焰从四肢升起
静如处女
静如霜后的北方
红叶满山
静如我初对你
静如我当年难以启齿说爱
静如我死后一百年

折箭为誓
指天为誓
或者以死为誓
何如默默无言

我真的以为
最完美、最高尚的是
静静的火焰么？

1992.5.17

大自然咏叹调

秋风四起
雍容华贵的落叶就像
我纯洁的身体

大自然
把你广阔的森林种在我的血上
草地种在我的天堂
在我的前额种植你的阳光
给我长久幸福的只有你——
夜半歌声
绿色的葡萄酒
日夜携手的情人
把我含在口里

大自然，穿上你的水晶鞋
我日夜舞蹈
我是大自然有灵的人
谁能破译
谁能洞烛其奸
谁就能东山再起

蓝色多瑙河正是花开时节
月上中天
照耀着坚强的男子汉
有谁比失魂落魄的狼
更加忧伤
没有国界的风
没有国籍的鸟
是上帝的千里鹅毛

淫雨霏霏
心中布满泥泞
何时焚风四起

凤凰火起
我是穿裤子的云，大笑着
葬身自然

1991.12.20

大雨

雨中沐浴的女人
洪荒中的女人
肋骨冒着新鲜的热气

她想，是的
野兽们正安居乐业
每棵树都很温柔，不分性别
像大雨中站在情人的窗口
不，她们是绝望的伟人
结束了世代无休的争论

让那个深色的男人走开
让女王乘雨车独自徘徊
不朽的痕迹
在雨中显现出来
显现出来

1991.12.23

当生活流逝

当生活流逝，
只有记忆永恒，
当记忆流逝，
有一些物质
为精神作证！

2002.2.17

妈妈——

妈妈——
你安然坐在远方的云中
你的身边似有上帝的空位

妈妈——
我做了一个梦
你在梦中不断地复生
于是我夜夜等待着你
变成美丽的鬼归来

妈妈——
在清晨好像有你起床的味道
在深夜又传来你洗涤毛巾的声音
这个世界，处处有你的温热
这个大地，铺满了你织绣的花纹
你为我的命运而忧愁，直到白发
你哭泣，像十七岁的少女

妈妈——
失去了你，生活变得如此坚硬
空气失去了弹性
生命啊，是如此的空洞
我的手从没有如此贪婪
只想抚摸你温暖的身体
我的眼睛从没有如此疯狂
要在茫茫人海中找到一个你
我相信上天有灵，大地有知
我相信灵魂不散，死而复生

妈妈——
你丰满柔润，像圆满的果实
你已随风而去，像星球游走太空

我祈祷每年有一天我们能相见
我能在水中找到你纯洁的眼睛

妈妈——
你为什么曾经存在而不永远存在
我此生唯一的悲剧
就是不能终生与你同行

妈妈——
我看见你坐在云中
望着这个再也不能落脚的城市
从此，我只能对着天空喊——妈妈！
从此，你是我举头可见的神灵——

2002.5

天地人歌

——题一莲绘画《仙乐飘飘》

草叶为美目
百果为香唇
天使伸千手
雨露自生根

万物常相思
水火亦相容
天地有相合
人子且长歌

千花迭次开
沧海又桑田
人为神，魂为仙
清静起舞的云中莲

2008.05.16
5.12大地震后第五天

致观众

　　——写在诗人画展开幕之日

（一）

2012，预言，预言，预言……
而人类百口莫辩
试想，是否要抢劫
上帝抛出的最后一枚小钱

人类自知罪孽深重
香火明灭许下亿万个心愿
而欲望像坏了闸的跑车
沿悬崖飞驰

（二）

谁的手能洗净心灵？
谁的目光可把未来洞穿？
谁的想象能猜中上帝的意图？
谁的善心可化解危难？

谁能啊
谁能啊
谁能让贪婪的人类停止杀戮
与众生平等结缘？

诗人啊，如果你还能活一年
你是否可做此事？
如果你还能活一天
你是否可描述这个答案？

（三）

是的，今天——2012初始
诗人的答案封在这彩色的迷宫
谁能穿过火焰取到钥匙
从地狱这边到地狱那边？

你啊，看到光了吗？
看到光了吗？
请耐心些，再耐心些，寻找
直到"你妈喊你回家吃饭"……

2012.元月

带王冠的玫瑰

令真理丑陋
光荣暗淡的玫瑰
带王冠的玫瑰
装饰延绵不绝的岁月
给人永不毁灭的欲望

2017

附注

《黄果树大瀑布》
黄果树大瀑布位于中国贵州省，是东亚最大的瀑布之一。

《情舞》
第九小节：原诗中"带电的肉体"参考惠特曼诗作"I Sing the Body Electric."译本将其替换为惠特曼诗作"Song of Myself"中的"You villain touch! what are you doing?"

《独身女人的卧室》
第九小节："Ah, linger on, thou art so fair!"（原诗中此句为"请停留一下"）出自歌德作品《浮士德》中浮士德与魔鬼的打赌。

《被围困者》
王子裤与巴拿马裤是流行于二十世纪八十年代中国的健美裤。

《噩梦》
迈克尔·塞维特斯，西班牙文艺复兴时期人文主义者，1553年在日内瓦因异端罪被绑在火刑柱上烧死。

《夏》
第四小节：原诗中"四面楚歌"源自一则中国成语，用于描述被敌人围困的场景。译本中被译为"I'm surrounded by a chorus of my enemies"。

《大自然咏叹调》
原诗中"千里鹅毛"源自一则中国唐朝故事，寓意礼物虽轻却代表很重的情谊。译本中被译为"small gifts / Laden with love's intentions"。

《天地人歌》
"沧海又桑田"是一句中国习语，描述时间的推移带给世界的巨大变迁。

YI LEI (伊蕾), born Sun Gui-zhen in Tianjin, China, in 1951, was one of the most influential figures of Chinese poetry in the 1980s. Sent to the countryside to work on a farm in 1969, two years later she became a reporter for the Liberation Army and a staff member of the newspaper the *Railway Corps*. Yi Lei studied creative writing at the Lu Xun Academy, and earned a BA in Chinese literature from Peking University. In 1991, she moved to Moscow, where she lived and wrote for a number of years. She published eight collections of poems, among them *A Single Woman's Bedroom*, *The Love Poems of Yi Lei*, *Women's Age*, and *Selected Poems of Yi Lei*. A recipient of the Zhuang Zhongwen Literature Prize, Yi Lei's work has been translated into English, Japanese, French, Italian, and Russian. She died in 2018.

TRACY K. SMITH is the author of four collections of poetry, including *Wade in the Water* and *Life on Mars*, winner of the Pulitzer Prize. She is also the author of a memoir, *Ordinary Light*, which was a finalist for the National Book Award. Smith served as the twenty-second Poet Laureate of the United States. She teaches at Princeton University and lives in New Jersey.

CHANGTAI BI, born in Tianjin, China, is a poetry translator from China who is currently a university teacher. He was responsible for the first draft of the English translation of *Selected Poems of Yi Lei*.

The text of *My Name Will Grow Wide Like a Tree* is set in Arno Pro.
Book design by Rachel Holscher.
Composition by Bookmobile Design and Digital Publisher Services,
Minneapolis, Minnesota.
Manufactured by Friesens on acid-free, 100 percent
postconsumer wastepaper.